MW00634809

Redemptive History
for the
Rest of Us

Part 2: Kings to Malachi

Frederica R Jones

Cover design: Ying Liu

ISBN: 978-0-9885565-2-2

Admont Publishing - www.admontpublishing.com

1R

1. Table of Contents

Introduction

The Bible is one book telling one story. This is God's Story from the beginning — creation, to the final restoration when Jesus Christ returns to reign forever over a perfect Universe. The first two chapters of Genesis tell of the Universe created in perfection. The last two chapters of Revelation tell of the Universe redeemed and restored to perfection. Between these bookends is the explanation of what caused the perfect creation to fall into corruption, evil, sin and decay. It also documents God's unfolding plan of how He intends to restore and redeem His creation, and bring some from every nation, from all tribes, and peoples and languages to worship and praise Him forever.

God doesn't change. The God of the Old Testament is the same God of the New Testament: "Jesus Christ is the same yesterday and today and forever" (Hebrews 13:8, NIV). This same God described His character to Moses:

> The LORD, the LORD, the compassionate and gracious God, slow to anger, abounding in love and faithfulness, maintaining love to thousands, and forgiving wickedness, rebellion and sin. Yet he does not leave the guilty unpunished… (Exodus 34:6-7, NIV).

The book is divided into the Old Testament—history before Jesus lived on earth—and the New Testament—history of Jesus' life, death resurrection and ascension. Further, the New Testament covers the history of the church after Jesus' ascension and the promise of His second coming when all again will be set right and the entire Universe will live in a redeemed state to praise and honor Him.

The Old Testament is comprised of historical books, wisdom literature and the books of the prophets. The New Testament gives four views of Jesus' life, a history of the early church during the life of the Apostles and letters written to the early churches advising us how to live.

This study is designed to give an overview of Scripture — the action parts of the Bible. The story line is exciting and riveting for it describes real people in real life all told with the oversight of our loving, sovereign Creator. The Law, Wisdom Books and the bulk of the books of the prophets are all very important but when the framework is comprehended first, the rest can then be more easily put into place in our reading and understanding.

After Jesus' crucifixion, two men were dejectedly walking away from Jerusalem on the road to Emmaus when the risen Lord Jesus joined them. However, they did not recognize Him. Jesus asks why they are so disturbed and they tell this 'stranger' about Jesus of Nazareth.

> He was a prophet, powerful in word and deed before God and all the people. The chief priests and our rulers handed him over to be sentenced to death, and they crucified him; but we had hoped that he was the one who was going to redeem Israel...(Luke 24:19-21, NIV).

Jesus replies:

> How foolish you are, and how slow to believe all that the prophets have spoken! Did not the Messiah have to suffer these things and then enter his glory? And beginning with Moses and all the Prophets, he explained to them what was said in all the Scriptures concerning himself (Luke 24:25-27).

Don't you wish that lecture of Jesus was given to us? That we could read exactly what He told these two men?

Well, we have it — it's called The Bible. Thus we will take time after each book of the Old Testament to look for some of the places where we see Jesus in the story, for it is about Him. He is the main character and to Him belongs all the glory and thanksgiving for making His history, our history and graciously including us in His plan of redemption and salvation; and our story, like His story will continue throughout all of eternity.

In Part One of "Redemptive History for the Rest of Us" the story from the beginning through the reign of King David was studied. At the beginning of the Story, God's Story, we saw that God created all that is and it was very good. However, humanity represented by Adam and Eve, thought they knew better than God. They rejected God's clear command, even having been warned of the consequence of such behavior, thus enslaving themselves to Satan. From that point, evil spread very rapidly.

By the time of Noah we are told:

The LORD saw how great the wickedness of the human race had become on the earth, and that every inclination of the thoughts of the human heart was only evil all the time. (Genesis 6:5, NIV).

And God sent the Flood, in a way to start again. However, the heart of humanity had not been changed—evil and sin still reigned. The human race then attempted to "make a name for themselves." They began to build a tower to try to get to God. Their efforts were foiled and languages confused making it very much more difficult to work together.

Then God began to work with one man, promising: "I will make you into a great nation, and I will bless you; I will make your name great, and you will be a blessing" to all nations. Notice that if we trust God, He will make our name great—we can't do that. The people of Babel found that out. But Abraham, we're told, "believed God and it was credited to him as righteousness."

Throughout all of the forgoing, God was making His ultimate plan a bit clearer: first an enigmatic promise that someone would come to deal with Satan. By the time of Abraham, we get a shadowy idea of a substitute who will take our punishment. These blessings and promises are passed from

Abraham to Isaac to Jacob. Jacob fathers 12 sons who are the origin of the nation of Israel.

Jacob's son Joseph, through adversity ends up in Egypt—going from a slave, to a prisoner, to the prime minister. It is through Joseph that many are saved from a mammoth area wide famine. Joseph models remarkable Christ-like forgiveness of the wrong done to him. All of his family (the Hebrews) moved to a remote section of Egypt where they are protected and isolated from 'the world's ways.' Thus they are able to prosper and multiply greatly.

Four hundred years after the close of Genesis, an Egyptian ruler who did not know Joseph came to leadership in Egypt. The Hebrews became slaves with arduous labor required of them. Even though Pharaoh had ruled that all male babies should be killed, Moses is born. Through amazing circumstances he is saved from death and brought up in the court of Pharaoh.

By age forty, he is ready to identify himself with 'his people'—the Hebrews. He goes about this in a way that gets him exiled into the wilderness for 40 years to tend sheep. At age 80 God appears to him and commissions Moses to lead the Hebrews—God's people—out of Egypt and ultimately into Canaan—the land promised to Abraham. (See Genesis 13:14-15; Genesis 15:18-21).

Through many trials, afflictions and rebellions, Moses does lead them out of Egypt to the threshold of The Promised Land. However because of one rather huge act of disobedience, Moses is refused entrance into Canaan at the time the rest of the Hebrew Nation goes in.

However, because of the grace and forgiveness of Christ Jesus Moses does go into the Promised Land in the company of Jesus (Matthew 17:1-3). This should be great encouragement to us; though the consequence of our disobedience may thwart out desires in the moment, ultimately, if we confess and repent of our sin, love and trust Jesus we will be taken to be with Him in The Promised Land. There the deepest desires of our hearts will be satisfied.

It is after Moses' death that Joshua leads the Hebrews into Canaan. The Israelites conquer some of the land God promised to give them, but many of those dwelling in the land are left to co-exist with them. Coexistence often meant syncretism and apostasy as Israel tried to fit in with the other nations rather than remaining faithful to the LORD as they promised Joshua they would do.

After settling into Canaan and Joshua's death the people begin to take on the ways of 'the world' and a cycle ensues: the people rebel, God gives them over to their rebellious hearts, enemies oppress them, they cry out to God for Mercy, God responds and gives them a Judge to lead them back to right living. They remain at peace through the lifetime of the judge. However, again and again, after the death of the judge the cycle repeats —"And the people of Israel again did what was evil in the sight of the Lord…" (Judges 4:1)

After many iterations of this cycle the last judge and first prophet—Samuel is born. By this time the people want to be like every other nation and demand a king. They realize that they need someone to lead and guide them, but rather than turning to THE KING, they demand an earthly king. Samuel warns them of some of the more severe consequences of earthly kingships but the people are not dissuaded. Led by God, Samuel anoints Israel's first king—Saul. Saul starts his reign as a 'good' king, delivering Israel from some of their enemies. However, Saul becomes self-serving, arrogant and completely turns away from trusting God.

Samuel is then commissioned to anoint David to be king. David's kingship is long and arduously won. Saul becomes jealous of David and pursues him all over the kingdom trying to kill him. However God protects David and he does, eventually, become Israel's king. David is one of the most revered kings of Israel. But, alas, not the perfect King we need. After David's enemies have been defeated, great wealth acquired, and everything one could want given to him, it seems he became complacent.

Thus in the spring of the year, David, perhaps bored, and without new challenges, sent all his friends and advisors away to war. Always before David went with his troops. Now, alone in the palace and guided by what he sees, ignoring what he knows is right, he reaches out to take what is not his; he commits adultery and tried to cover that by having the husband of Bathsheba murdered.

Why is David known as a man after God's own heart? Certainly one reason is his humility. Immediately after being convicted of gross sin by the prophet Nathan, David admits all he has done: "I have sinned against the LORD." But even though forgiven the consequences are enormous: four of David's son's are killed and the kingdom, which reached its zenith under David's rule, begins a slow slide toward exile from the land of promise.

Now a few words about the particulars of this workbook:

- This workbook—part two in a series of three—picks up the story in 1 Kings, as King David is close to death and his successor is a matter of some contention. Once that question is settled, we will follow the story through Solomon's reign, split of the kingdom into the Northern and Southern kingdoms, into exile and back to the Promised Land.

- The last question in each chapter is asking for you to try to identify where Jesus is either prefigured or pointed to through similarities, contrasts, symbols, foreshadows or types. This is followed by a section entitled "What do we learn about Jesus..."— this is not intended to be an exhaustive list.

- This is different in Chapter 10—Malachi. The last question in chapter 10 gives several references. This question is a review and asks you to document the emerging picture in the Old Testament, of Jesus our Messiah, King and Lord.

- The section entitled: "Redemptive History through..." is an overview of the mega story; updated book by book; intended as a review of the story and anticipation of what's to come.

- The questions are designed to drive the story forward. Most are content questions: what, why, when, where. Some are thought questions where you will be challenged to think of the broader view. These questions have *** at the beginning and usually have no direct chapter and verse(s) cited. Some questions are either stated or implied application questions.

- If you find your time very limited, the most important part of this study is to READ! If you have never read through the Bible, this is an opportunity to read through the 'action' parts of the Bible, to get an understanding of the framework. Following is a listing of that reading. Book, chapters and verses reference the action parts. If you don't have time to work with the questions, try very hard to at least keep reading!

My hope is that through this study each person will gather an understanding of the story line or framework of the Bible: either a beginning framework or adding to your emerging understanding of God's story. Study of Scripture is a lifetime activity: simple enough for the beginner to understand and deep enough for the greatest minds to continue to probe. My prayer is that each of us would be like the men on the Road to Emmaus; that He would draw us into conversation, teach us His Word, and disclose Himself as the risen Savior. [1]

And may it all be to the Glory of our Lord and King without whom we would have no story (Bible) and no ultimate hope or knowledge of His promise to us — eternal life (1 John 2:25).

---

[1] *Tabletalk Magazine,* Ligonier Ministries, August, 2015, 54.

Redemptive History Reading List

Kings through Malachi

1 Kings
    Chapters
1—3	David and Solomon—United Kingdom
4:29—6:1	Solomon's Wisdom and Temple Building
7:51—10:13	Solomon's godly Reign
11—22	Solomon's failing - People Rebel – Kingdom Splits

2 Kings
1—14	Prophets and Kings

Jonah
1—4	Repentance and Retraction of Doom

2 Kings
15—25	End of Northern Kingdom; Exile of Judah (Isaiah 6; 26; 36—39; Jeremiah 1)

2 Chronicles
36:22-23	God works through a Pagan King (Jeremiah 29:10-14)

Daniel
1—6	Those Who Truly Trust God

Esther
1—9	He works Behind The Scenes

Ezra
1:1-8	Those First to Return
2:68—6:22	Building and Opposition
7:1-28	Ezra Comes to Jerusalem
8:15—10:17	Problem with marriage

Nehemiah
1—6	Building the Jerusalem Wall—Opposition

Malachi
1—4	Last Words from the Old Testament

Chapter 1

1 Kings: The Beginning of the End

1 Kings

"Listen! A farmer went out to sow his seed... Other seed
fell among thorns, which grew up and choked the plants,
so that they did not bear grain"
(Mark 4:3,7, NIV).

Sin has painful consequences. Although David, truly repentant, was immediately forgiven following his adultery, the consequences inevitably followed. The kingdom that reached its zenith under David's rule, begins a slow slide toward exile from the land of promise. After David, kingship passes to Solomon, then under Rehoboam, Solomon's son, the kingdom splits into two—Northern (Israel) and Southern (Judah). In these chapters we see the first part of this deteriorating slide as well as the work of God-sent Prophets in forth telling (what has God said) and foretelling (what is to come).

Questions to ponder as you read the text:

1. 1 Kings 1:1 tells us: "When King David was old and well advanced in years," one of his sons decided he should be king. Who was that? (1 kings 1:5).

2. Was he King David's choice? (1 Kings 1:28-30).

3. What do we learn about Solomon's heart at the beginning of his reign? (1 Kings 3:5-14).

4. What was the cause of Solomon's turn away from faithfulness to the Lord? (1 Kings 11:1-6).

5. Solomon's son Rehoboam succeeded him as king. What happened to the 'United Kingdom' at the beginning of Rehoboam's reign? (1 Kings 12:1-17, 22-24).

6. See the chart on page 72 listing all the Kings of Israel (Northern Kingdom) and Judah (Southern Kingdom). From Saul through King Ahab fill in what you can on this chart. (The Northern Kingdom is sometimes referred to as "Ephraim").

7. It was always God's intent that a king would ultimately rule Israel. (Genesis 17:6, 16; Genesis 35:11; Genesis 49:10 and Deuteronomy 17:14-20 where instruction is given for the conduct of the kings). However an earthly king, for better or worse, only foreshadows The King—Jesus. Earthly kings, like the judges, will be flawed. In 1 Samuel 8:10-18 the Prophet Samuel warned the Hebrews as to what it would be like to live under an earthly king. Identify some of these consequences: 1 Kings 4:27-28; 1 Kings 5:13; 1 Kings 9:15 and 1 Kings 12:4.

8. Jeremiah 7:25 tells us how God continually confronted the Israelites with His call on their lives: "From the time your ancestors left Egypt until now, day after day, again and again I sent you my servants the prophets." Now we see the Prophet Elijah in a dramatic confrontation. What was this confrontation about? (1 Kings 18:19-39).

9. Elijah had just witnessed the magnificent power and might of the LORD. Why did Elijah run? (1 Kings 19:1-4).

10. How did God comfort Elijah? (1 Kings 19:5-9).

11. What three things did God commission Elijah to do? (1 Kings 19:15-16).

12. To get a flavor of King Ahab and his wife Jezebel read 1 Kings 21:1-15. After Naboth's murder what messages did God give Elijah to tell King Ahab? (1 Kings 21:17-26).

Did Elijah's predictions about Ahab and Jezebel come true? (1 Kings 22:37-38; 2 Kings 9:30-37).

13. What was Ahab's response to Elijah's prophecies—question 12? (1 Kings 21:27).

14. What changed as a result of Ahab's attitude? (1 Kings 21:28-29).

15. ***As you reflect on the Scripture from this section, do you note any hint, type, or foreshadow of Jesus Christ?

NOTES

What do we learn about Jesus in this section of Scripture?

- **Solomon and Wisdom**
  At the beginning of Solomon's reign Solomon asks for and God grants him wisdom—His Wisdom; Solomon's wise rule points toward the One in whom perfect wisdom dwells—Jesus.
  Proverbs 8:35 reads: "For those who find me [wisdom] find life and receive favor from the LORD." This was true for Solomon as long as he allowed wisdom to govern his life and reign. But when he eschewed wisdom and turned to his own way then Proverbs 8:36 described his later reign: "But those who fail to find me [wisdom] harm themselves; all who hate me love death" (NIV).

  Unlike Solomon, the revelation of Jesus Christ as the wisdom of God (John 1:1-18) shows us the value of God's wisdom in our lives. How do we "get this wisdom?" We "get this wisdom" through study of His Word—The Bible.

- **Elijah Raises the Dead**
  Elijah brings the son of a widow back to life. This resurrection and others we read about in the Old Testament points forward to Jesus Christ; He has the power to bring life from death. He granted this power to Elijah.

- **Elijah is comforted**
  The tender mercies of Jesus are ministered to Elijah when he is deeply discouraged. After an overwhelming victory over the prophets of Baal on Mount Carmel, Elijah, terrified by Queen Jezebel, runs for his life. He pleads with God to take his life—he is that discouraged. Instead God sends an angel to feed, quench his thirst, and provide a deeply restful sleep. After rest and nourishment God re-commissions him and sends him on his way—refreshed in the Lord.

- **Jesus – Lord of Mercy following Repentance**
  After the murder of the "innocent" Naboth and the outright

6

stealing of his property, Elijah confronts and condemns Ahab with God's promised judgment upon him and his wife Jezebel. However, Ahab listens and humbles himself—for a time—and God holds off His judgment: "...I will not bring this disaster in his day, but I will bring it on his house in the days of his son" (I Kings 21:29).

Michael Griffiths comments "God's judgments, even if prophesied, can be averted by genuine repentance."[2] We'll see this principle at work again.

---

[2] Michael C. Griffiths, *Jonah,* The International Bible Commentary, *F.F. Bruce,* gen. ed. (Zondervan, 1986), 917.

Chapter 2

Kings and Prophets: Rebellion and God's Call

2 Kings Chapters 1-14

"There was a man who had two sons. He went to the first
and said, 'Son, go and work today in the vineyard.' 'I will
not,' he answered, but later he changed his mind and went.
Then the father went to the other son and said the same
thing. He answered, 'I will, sir,' but he did not go. Which of
the two did what his father wanted?"
(Matthew 21:28-31a, NIV).

In these chapters we see a series of "good" and "bad" kings ruling
in the two kingdoms that comprised Israel (Northern and Southern). God
also raised up prophets. The prophets delivered verbal messages, signs
and object lessons—visibly depicting God's message. This is called forth
telling. Along with forth telling the prophets also fore-told what would
happen if the people were not repentant—humbling their hearts before
the LORD and returning to true worship of the King of Heaven and Earth.

Questions to ponder as you read the test:

1. Elisha mainly ministered as a prophet to the Northern Kingdom. List
   some of the high lights of Elisha's years as God's prophet to Israel.
   2 Kings 2:11-12

   2 Kings 4:1-7

2 Kings 4:32-37

2 Kings 5:1-14

2 Kings 6:8-18

2 Kings 9:1-3

2. To whom was King Jehoram (King in Judah) married? (2 Kings 8:18).

3. King Jehoram's son is King Ahaziah. Who was the mother of King Ahaziah—king in Judah? (2 Kings 8:26)

   See also the chart on page 74 The Genealogy of the Kings of Israel and Judah." Find Athaliah, Jehoram and Ahaziah (all of Judah). This will allow you to better understand the relationships of these people to King Ahab —king in Israel.

4. What kind of a grandmother was Athaliah? (2 Kings 11:1-3).

5. Jehu was commissioned to purify Israel. After all his "purifying" does Jehu have a heart to follow the Lord? (2 Kings 10:30-31).

6. Fill in the Kings Chart from Jehoshaphat through Jeroboam II. (page 72).

7. ***As you reflect on the Scripture from this section, do you note any hint, type, or foreshadow of Jesus Christ?

NOTES

What do we learn about Jesus in these chapters of 2 Kings?

- **Elijah Taken Up – 2 Kings 2**
  Elijah was one of only two people who left earth without dying, pointing forward to Jesus' second coming. The Apostle Paul puts it this way in 1 Thessalonians 4:16-18:

  > For the Lord himself will come down from heaven, with a
  > loud command, with the voice of the archangel and with
  > the trumpet call of God, and the dead in Christ will rise
  > first. After that, we who are still alive and are left will be
  > caught up together with them in the clouds to meet the
  > Lord in the air. And so we will be with the Lord forever.

- **Miracles of Elisha**
  Elisha performed many and varied miracles all used by God to authenticate his ministry as one sent by God. Miracles point toward Christ the ultimate miracle worker—the One able to work outside the usual laws of nature.

- **King Jehu – Contrast to King Jesus**
  Jehu commissioned and empowered by the LORD to lead people back to God but he, unlike our King Jesus utterly failed to be led by the LORD.

Redemptive History through 2 Kings Chapter 14

As King David grew old and approached death there was a scramble as to who was going to succeed him as king. Adonijah set himself up as king but this was not David—nor the Lord's intent. Solomon was the rightful heir to the throne.

Solomon started his reign in an honest, humble fashion. God appeared to him in a dream, "Ask for whatever you want me to give you." Solomon asked for wisdom and the early part of his reign reflected God's wisdom. However 1 Kings 3:1-3 foreshadow his departure from the wisdom of the Lord: marrying for political alliance and offering sacrifices and burning incense on the high places.

High places were mainly shrines furnished with idols and various other objects dedicated to pagan deities.

> These places posed a threat to the pure worship of
> Yahweh, and after the building of the central temple in
> Jerusalem most references to them are pejorative, for they
> represented conflicting loyalty and competing
> allegiance...Beginning with Solomon's reign, the toleration
> of high places led to syncretistic worship [incorporation of
> different religions, cultures and thought] and apostasy
> [abandonment of belief]. [3]

One would have to give a mixed review to Solomon's reign. The end of his life tells us that Solomon had married many foreign women who "turned his heart after other gods. His heart was not fully devoted to the LORD his God, as the heart of David his father had been" (1 Kings 11:4).

---

[3] Donald J. Wiseman, *1 & 2 Kings,* Tyndale Old Testament Commentaries 9 (Downers Grove, Illinois: Inter-Varsity Press, 1993), 83.

After Solomon's death his son Rehoboam succeeds him. By this time the people had suffered many of the afflictions about which the Prophet Samuel warned when they insisted on having a king. The people said, "Your father put a heavy yoke on us, but now lighten the harsh labor and the heavy yoke he put on us, and we will serve you." Rehoboam's reply, "My father made your yoke heavy; I will make it even heavier..." (1 Kings 12:14). This precipitated a revolt and a split in the kingdom into the Northern Kingdom—Israel or Ephraim and the Southern Kingdom—Judah.

The remainder of the Books of The Kings (1st and 2nd Kings) lines out the reigns of the various kings of both kingdoms: the North (Israel) and the South (Judah). Some were commended for doing what was right in the eyes of the Lord but most did what was evil—perpetuating the ultimate demise of both kingdoms.

Throughout all of this history we read about God's continued wooing of His people through the prophets—wooing them back to righteous living. A calling which they predominately ignored.

In the Books of the Kings we've read about the ministry of Elijah and Elisha. Elijah plays a very dramatic role when he summoned all the prophets of Baal to a confrontation on Mount Carmel (1 Kings 18). Elijah asked the gathered people "How long will you waver between two opinions? If the LORD is God, follow him; but if Baal is God, follow him." The LORD "wins" and "When the people saw this, they fell prostrate and cried, 'The LORD—he is God! The LORD—he is God!'"

But alas, their response was very thin and their hearts were not changed. We also read about the Prophet Elisha and the many and varied miracles that were part of his ministry. These miracles proved that the Lord sent him to forth-tell the truth and remind Israel of the love of the One true God. (Forth-telling is reminding us of what God has said.)

During the reign of Jeroboam II (Northern Kingdom—Israel) God calls Jonah and dramatically demonstrates the connection between repentance and restoration.

Chapter 3

God Has A Plan For Our Lives

Jonah Chapters 1-4

Then Peter began to speak: "I now realize how true it is
that God does not show favoritism but accepts from every
nation the one who fears him and does what is right
(Acts 10:34-35, NIV).

Scholars find it quite likely that Jonah was called to prophecy to Nineveh—capital city of Assyria—during the reign of Jereboam II, king in Israel. This was a period of Assyrian weakness when they were being threatened by enemies from the north and fearful of total defeat. Thus they were willing to listen to the message of Jonah. During this same time, Israel under King Jereboam II and Judah under King Uzziah aka: Azariah were enjoying a period of prosperity unknown since the days of Kings David and Solomon.

Although economically prosperous there was much social injustice in Israel. They were under the leadership of a king who was not a godly ruler. The lesson Jonah learned in Nineveh was a lesson Israel needed to learn also.

Questions to ponder as you read the test:

1. What did God commission Jonah to do? (Jonah 1:1-2).

2. What was Jonah's response to God's command? (Jonah 1:3).

3. ***Assyria was known in the ancient world as one of the cruelest of conquerors. Why might Jonah have wanted to disregard God's call?

4. (Personal reflection) What are some of the reasons you might cite to disregard God's call?

5. What was the effect of Jonah's story upon his fellow sailors? (Jonah 1:8-10).

6. ***Paraphrase Jonah's prayer (Jonah 2:1-9).

7. Does Jonah obey God's call the second time? (Jonah 3:1-3).

8. What was the response of the people of Nineveh to Jonah's warning? (Jonah 3:4-5).

9. How did God react to the response of the people of Nineveh? (Jonah 3:10).

10. Why was Jonah angry with the Lord? (Jonah 4:1-3).

11. **How does the Lord deal with Jonah's anger? (Jonah 4:5-11).

12. ***As you reflect on the Scripture from this section, do you note any hint, type, or foreshadow of Jesus Christ?

NOTES

What do we learn about Jesus in the Book of Jonah?

- **Sign of the Prophet Jonah – Matthew 12:39** [4]
  Both Jonah and Jesus offered their lives as a substitutionary sacrifice to save others (Jonah 1:11-12; Matthew 20:28).

  Both preached a message of repentance (Jonah 3:4; Mark 1:15).

  After three days both reappeared alive (Jonah 1:17; Jesus' resurrection).

  As a result of their ministries, repentant gentiles were delivered (Jonah 3:6-10; Matthew 8:13).

- **Authority over Nature**
  Both Jesus and Jonah were in a boat—asleep during a raging storm (Jonah 1:4, 15; Mark 4:37-39). Both Jonah and Jesus' disciples learned that "even the wind and the waves obey him!" [The LORD Jesus].

- **Prophesied Judgment Turned Back because of Repentance**
  In the mercy shown Nineveh we see again the truth of what Michael Griffiths said: "God's judgments, even if prophesied, can be averted by genuine repentance. " [5]

- **Jonah Learning the Lesson of Romans 2:4**
  It was hot in Nineveh and Jonah was very tired. God provided shade for Jonah but later destroyed it. Jonah was angry (Jonah 4:5-9). As the Ninavites learned about God's kindness, Jonah also needed to learn the lesson: "Or do you show contempt for the riches of his kindness, forbearance and patience, not realizing that God's kindness is intended to lead you to repentance?" (Romans 2:4, NIV).

---

[4] R.C. Sproul, "Jonah." *The Reformation Study Bible,* (2015) General editor R.C. Sproul. Orlando, Florida: Reformation Trust, 2014. 1562-1563.

[5] Griffiths, 917.

Redemptive History through Jonah

God used the call to Jonah to remind Israel that they were to be a blessing to all nations. At the very beginning of their history, God said that He would bless them but in turn they were to bless and be a blessing to others (Genesis 12:1-3). Jonah learns that God's grace and mercy extends to gentiles as well as Israelites.

Jonah also needed to learn that just because he was "one of God's chosen" that did not exempt him from humble and obedient living before the God of the Universe. Jonah observes a dramatic shift in the heart of the Ninivites. When confronted with Jonah's message: "confess and repent or you will be destroyed," they did just that. "When the news reached the King of Nineveh, he rose from his throne, took off his royal robes, covered himself with sackcloth and sat down in the dust." Then he called his people to "give up their evil ways and their violence." And "God had compassion and did not bring upon them the destruction he had threatened" (Jonah 3).

Jonah wanted Nineveh and the Assyrians to be destroyed; he did not appreciate the LORD's compassion. God worked on Jonah's heart through an object lesson—a vine and a worm (Jonah 4).

But again as we've seen so many times before, Ninivite repentance turned out to be only situational; their hearts were not changed. After Jonah's ministry, there was a rapid resurgence of Assyrian power leading to the decimation of Israel and it's total destruction in 722 BC. This was followed by a significant threat to Judah under the reign of Hezekiah in 701 BC.

How fast do we recognize our "way-ward" thoughts and behavior? How quickly do we confess and ask to be forgiven? When we repent is it situational or is it a genuine, lasting heart change? Of course a true heart change necessitates the activity of the Holy Spirit making it possible for us to truly change.

Chapter 4

Good Kings/Bad Kings —God's Call

2 Kings Chapters 15:1-21:18

but you must not eat from the tree
of the knowledge of good and evil, for when you eat from it
you will certainly die
(Genesis 2:17).

The above command and warning, given so long ago and yet repeated in one form or another again and again; God reminding us that if we obey we will be blessed but is we persist in disobedience we will be cursed. And so in these chapters we will read about the demise and total destruction—death of the Northern Kingdom—Israel, along with the reasons that they were "cursed". The question—will Judah learn from the fall of Israel?

Questions to ponder as you read the text:

1. Fill in the Kings Chart from Uzziah to Manasseh (page 72).

2. What happened to Israel—aka: Samaria? (2 Kings 17:5-6).

3. Why was Israel—Samaria—conquered? (2 Kings 17:7-12).

4. Was Israel warned of the consequences of disobedience? (Joshua 23:12-13; 2 Kings 17:13-14).
Who warned them?

How could they prevent the consequences?

What were the consequences?

5. What about us? The way we behave does not save us—Jesus' work on the cross saves us, but Jesus said: "If you love me, keep my commandments" (John 14:15). And Martin Luther added: "We are saved by faith alone, but the faith that saves is never alone." If we love Him, our behavior should more and more reflect Him (and when it doesn't, we need to confess and repent). Are we fairly warned about the consequence of our behavior if we continue to deliberately sin? (See 1 Corinthians 6:9-10; Hebrews 12:14).

6. How is the character of Hezekiah's reign described? (2 Kings 18:3-7).

7. Read 2 Kings 18:13-16 and 2 Kings 20:12-19. Do these responses of Hezekiah reflect one who wholly trusted God?

Compare the above responses to Hezekiah's response when Assyria continues to threaten (2 Kings 19:1-4).

8. King Hezekiah suffered a near fatal illness. Hezekiah prayed for healing—what happened? (2 Kings 20:4-6).

9. How old was Manasseh when his father Hezekiah died and he (Manasseh) began his reign? (2 Kings 21:1).

   **Read 2 Kings 21:1-9. Putting your answers to questions 7 and 8 together, do you see any implications?

10. What kings reigned during the time of the Prophet Isaiah's ministry in Judah? (Isaiah 1:1).

11. ***What was Isaiah's commission from the Lord? (Isaiah 6:9-10).

12. How "successful" was Isaiah's ministry to be? (Isaiah 6:11-12).

13. Manasseh was reputed to be one of the worst kings of Judah, following his father—one of the most faithful kings of Judah. Was his extreme unfaithfulness the last word we hear about Manasseh? (2 Chronicles 33:10-16).

Was Manasseh forgiven?

Did God reverse the consequences resulting from his very unfaithful rule? (2 Kings 23:26-27).

14. ***As you reflect on the Scripture from this section, do you note any hint, type, or foreshadow of Jesus Christ?

NOTES

What do we learn about Jesus in chapters 15-21 of 2 Kings?

- **Ears Closed - The Patience of Christ Jesus**

  When enslaved in Egypt God redeemed Israel and graciously brought them to the Promised Land. We read about their many rebellions throughout the wilderness wandering; how again and again they turned away from the LORD. In the book of Judges and so too during the reign of the kings they sinned against the LORD their God; they constantly turned to the worship of other things—not God. Finally they reaped what they sowed. Through many centuries they were warned but would not listen to the LORD.

- **Jesus Doesn't Force**

  Israel was given and reminded of God's standard again and again—warned of the consequence of disobedience but never forced. This might remind us of Jesus' encounter with the "rich young man." He asked Jesus what he needed to do to gain eternal life. Jesus answers him. But "When the young man heard this, he went away sad..."(Matthew 19:22). Note that Jesus didn't run after him and compromise His requirements. His Word is His Word.

- **Jesus the Healer**

  King Hezekiah suffers a "fatal illness." The Prophet Isaiah tells the king he is going to die. Hezekiah pleads with the LORD—the healer—and 15 years was added to his life. After those additional 15 years, Hezekiah dies.

  Jesus brought several people back to life after they had died—Lazarus being one. But each of the ones resurrected eventually died again. Different from Jesus' resurrection—He was raised from the dead never to face death again. He is the "firstborn among many brothers and sisters" (Romans 8:29). That is, we too

23

can look forward to being raised from the dead, never to face death again–not just a 15-year reprieve—but forever.

- **Trusting God Even When All Alone and Facing Death**

  In the final chapter of Hezekiah's life, as Assyria was bearing down on Jerusalem in what looked like an inevitable, colossal defeat, Hezekiah turned to the LORD and trusted Him alone for deliverance. Just as Jesus all through His life trusted His Father. Of particular note: in His ultimate distress on the cross Jesus quoted the beginning of Psalm 22, which goes on to say: "Do not be far from me, for trouble is near and there is no one to help" (Psalm 22:11). An amazingly prophetic resignation to God's will—to see it through to the end. He knew, and trusted, that it was the LORD's will to crush Him (Isaiah 53:10) and yet, Jesus also knew that the ultimate plan was for total victory—paying for sin, slaying death and Satan, all proved by His triumphant resurrection.

Chapter 5

The End Of The Kingdom—Exile

2 Kings Chapters 21:19—25:30

...But as the terebinth and oak leave stumps when they are
cut down, so the holy seed will be the stump in the land
(Isaiah 6:13, NIV).

Judah does not learn from Israel's demise; in fact the prophets, accuse them of being worse than Israel. Although there were some massive attempts at reform under King Josiah, it wasn't enough—the hearts of the people were corrupt and hardened. Never the less, God's faithful, compassionate patience has the last word. He remembers His promise that David's kingdom was indeed to be forever and would be renewed.

Questions to ponder as you read the text:

1. Finish the Kings Chart from Amon through Zedekiah (page 72).

2. Josiah was the last "good" king of Judah. Did his faithfulness change the Lord's intention for Judah? (2 Kings 23:26-27).

3. What kings reigned in Judah during the ministry of the Prophet Jeremiah? (Jeremiah 1:1-3).

4. What was Jeremiah's commission? (Jeremiah 1:10).

5. How did the king, other "prophets" and people of Judah respond to Jeremiah's words from the Lord?

   Jeremiah 26:7-9

   Jeremiah 36:1-3; 20-26

   Jeremiah 37:1-2

   Jeremiah 38:1-6

6. Read Jeremiah 28. An example of Jeremiah's "competition". What was Hananiah's message? How did Jeremiah respond? What happened to Hananiah?

7. What are some of the reasons given for the demise and exile of Judah to Babylon? (2 Chronicles 36:15-21).

8. Judah was defeated by the Babylonians and sent into exile in 586 BC. Read Isaiah 45 verses 1 and verses 4-6. Who is named here? Would this person be a faithful follower of the Lord?

Now read 2 Chronicles 36:22-23. What will that person do whom the Prophet Isaiah named?

9. **The decree from Cyrus king of Persia was given in 538 BC. Isaiah ministered from 740 – 701 BC. What does this tell you about our sovereign LORD?

10. What are some of the behaviors that differentiated the "good" kings from the "bad" kings? (2 Kings 18:3-6; 2 Kings 21:2-6).

11. ***How do these behaviors apply to us in our culture?

12. ***As you reflect on the Scripture from this section, do you note any hint, type, or foreshadow of Jesus Christ?

NOTES

What do we learn about Jesus in the concluding chapters of 2 Kings?

"It was because of the LORD's anger that all this happened to Jerusalem and Judah, and in the end he thrust them from his presence" (2 Kings 24:20, NIV).

Without true heart repentance, Judah was warned that their end would be just as that of Israel. There comes a time when the patience of God runs out. Compare the time when the exile of Judah approached to Jesus' words on "Psalm Sunday" as He rode down from the Mount of Olives, seeing Jerusalem spread out before him and knowing that their time for repentance had run out:

> O Jerusalem, Jerusalem, the city that kills the prophets and
> stones God's messengers! How often I have wanted to
> gather your children together as a hen protects her chicks
> beneath her wings, but you wouldn't let me
> (Luke 13:34, New Living Translation).

The pathos is palpable—we can feel the pain in the heart of Jesus. He recognizes that the time for repentance has past and judgment will inevitably follow. He is very patient and long suffering but His patience is not eternal. He calls us to repentance, He gives many chances to confess but if we continue in sin, He reminds us: "he does not leave the guilty unpunished..." (Exodus 34:7).

But God always gives reason for hope even in the midst of despair. In the case of the exile, there were several things, yet again, that God used to demonstrate His commitment to the promise of a future.

- Jeremiah sums this up in 29:11,

> "I know the plans I have for you," declares the LORD,
> "plans to prosper you and not to harm you, plans to give
> you hope and a future"(NIV).

- **Buy Property**
  With imminent exile on the horizon, God tells Jeremiah to buy property—symbolic of God's promise that exile is not the last word for Judah.

- **Jehoiachin's Release from Prison**
  Zedekiah was the last King of Judah. He was an uncle of Jehoiachin. Zekekiah's nephew—Jehoiachin was actually the last in the line of the Davidic kings (See "Genealogy of the Kings of Israel and Judah" on page 74). Jehiachin was taken into captivity to Babylon in 597 BC—11 years before the Fall of Jerusalem. At the time of the exile Stephen Dempster, quoting later Biblical texts, describes the nation of Israel—or what was left of it:

  > ...the nation is a stump, the tree having been axed to the ground (Isaiah 6:13); the vast multitudes of survivors are but a mass of dried-out bones in an exilic graveyard (Ezekiel 37), and perhaps the last hope, the line of David, is confined to a Babylonian prison. [6]

  But the last historic note (2 Kings 25:27-30) relates the release of Jehoiachin, "promising hope for the kingdom of God." [7] The Davidic line will continue and culminate in Jesus Christ because the LORD made this a promise to King David (2 Samuel 7:ff16).

- **The Long Ago Prophecy about a Persian King**
  As 2 Kings ends with the hopeful note of King Jehoiachin being released from Babylonian prison, 2 Chronicles ends the same history with a hopeful note of a prophecy; prophecy from Isaiah some 200 years earlier about a Persian King—not yet born. This king would release Israel from captivity, allowing them to return to the land.

  Jesus knew the plans He had for Israel and they were plans to prosper and not to harm.

---

[6] Stephen G. Dempster, *Dominion and Dynasty A theology of the Hebrew Bible* (Downers Grove, Illinois: InterVarsity Press, 2003), 153.

[7] Ibid. , 233.

Redemptive History to the Time of the Exile

Hezekiah probably came to the throne in the waning years of the Northern Kingdom. It is noted about King Hezekiah, that:

> He did what was right in the eyes of the LORD, just as his
> father David had done...There was no one like him among
> all the kings of Judah, either before him or after him
> (2 Kings 18:3,5 - NIV).

Hezekiah and Josiah, ruling in the latter years of the monarchy, were two of the best kings to reign in Judah. Hezekiah was the only king to completely remove the "high places" (See explanation of "high places" on page 12). Both Hezekiah and Josiah—the last "good" king, undertook significant purification of religious practices.

Manasseh, born during the 15 years of extended life granted to Hezekiah was one of the worst kings of Judah. He systematically reversed all the "good" that his father, King Hezekiah, had done. The description of the reign of Manasseh:

> He did evil in the eyes of the LORD, following the
> detestable practices of the nations the LORD had driven
> out before the Israelites. He rebuilt the high places his
> father Hezekiah had destroyed; he also erected alters to
> Baal ...He bowed down to all the starry hosts and
> worshiped them...(2 Kings 21:2-3, NIV).

However, Manasseh was taken into captivity, suffered greatly and in his distress, turned to the LORD. His was a genuine repentance and God was merciful to him, restoring much that he lost in captivity; undergirding the principle that God is merciful and forgives us our sins if we have a true heart change (1 John 1:9).

Manasseh's life demonstrates another principle—the seriousness of sin; though forgiven, the consequences of his many sins were not obliterated; even given the "good" leadership of Josiah, Manasseh's grandson. No, the time for repentance had past and nothing could reverse it,

> Nevertheless, the LORD did not turn away from the heat of his fierce anger, which burned against Judah because of all that Manasseh had done to arouse his anger. So the LORD said, "I will remove Judah also from my presence as I removed Israel, and I will reject Jerusalem, the city I chose, and this temple, about which I said, 'My Name shall be there'" (2 Kings 23:26-27, NIV).

From King Josiah, the last "good king" it was a steady downhill of evil, syncretism and apostasy to the last faith-less king—Zedekiah.

And when the unbelievable happened and the Jews were taken into exile in Babylon one can feel their agony as expressed by the Psalmist in Psalm 137:1-6

> By the rivers of Babylon we sat and wept
> when we remembered Zion.
> There on the poplars
> we hung our harps,
> for there our captors asked us for songs,
> our tormentors demanded songs of joy;
> they said, "Sing us one of the songs of Zion!"
> How can we sing the songs of the Lord
> while in a foreign land?
> If I forget you, Jerusalem,
> may my right hand forget its skill.
> May my tongue cling to the roof of my mouth
> if I do not remember you,
> if I do not consider Jerusalem
> my highest joy.

Chapter 6

How To Live In A Hostile Culture

Daniel Chapters 1-6

Let us hold unswervingly to the hope we profess, for he
who promised is faithful. And let us consider how we may
spur one another on toward love and good deeds...
(Hebrews 10:23-24, NIV).

King Nebuchadnezzar took Daniel and his friends to Babylon in
605 BC—19 years before the destruction of Jerusalem and exile for the
rest of the Jews. Do Daniel and his friends demonstrate faith in the midst
of persecution? Can we learn from their courage? They indeed
demonstrated the command to Joshua: be strong and of good courage "for
the Lord your God will be with you wherever you go" (Joshua 1:9).

QUESTIONS TO PONDER AS YOU READ THE TEXT:

1. When Daniel was taken to Babylon, which Judean King was ruling?
   (Daniel 1:1-4).

2. What was the first act of Daniel and his friends that showed their trust
   in the Lord? (Daniel 1:8-14).

3. How did Daniel come to the attention of King Nebuchadnezzar?
   (Daniel 2:14-16, 24-25).

4. Whom does Daniel credit for the revelation and interpretation of King Nebuchadnezzar's dream? (Daniel 2:26-28).

5. Probably in response to his dream (chapter 2), King Nebuchadnezzar made an image (statue), set it up and required all people to bow down and worship the image or be thrown into the blazing furnace. How did Daniel's friends respond to this? (Daniel 3:8-12).

6. King Nebuchadnezzar is furious with rage and calls Shadrach, Meshach and Abednego before him to threaten that if they don't obey they will burn. What is their reply to the king? (Daniel 3:16-18).

7. They are thrown into the furnace – do they burn? (Daniel 3:24-25).

8. How did King Nebuchadnezzar's attitude change—at least for the time? (Daniel 3:28-30).

9. Daniel is called by King Nebuchadnezzar to interpret another of his dreams. What is the interpretation of this dream? (Daniel 4:20-26).

10. In order to avoid the dream's fulfillment what did King Nebuchadnezzar need to do? (Daniel 4:27).

11. King Nebuchadnezzar does not confess his sin nor renounce his arrogance so the dream is fulfilled. What is the outcome? (Daniel 4:36-37).

12. What edict did those hostile to and jealous of Daniel get King Darius to enact? (Daniel 6:6-7).

13. How did Daniel "get caught?" (Daniel 6:10-11).

What habits am I developing that would show the world that I follow Christ Jesus?

14. Because the edict had been signed it could not be revoked. Even though King Darius wanted to protect Daniel—he couldn't and Daniel is thrown to the lions. How does the story end? (Daniel 6:19-24).

15. ***We are living in an increasingly hostile culture—particularly hostile to God's Word. From the events reviewed in this book—Daniel—what are the take always for you?

16. ***As you reflect on the Scripture from this section, do you note any hint, type, or foreshadow of Jesus Christ?

NOTES

What do we learn about Jesus from the Book of Daniel?

It is very clear that Jesus is present in the lives of Daniel and his three friends:

- **Dream and Sign interpretation**
  Chapters 2 and 4 tell of Daniel's ability to interpret dreams. In Daniel 2:28 Daniel explains to the king that his ability is not his "but there is a God in heaven who reveals mysteries." In Chapter 5 Daniel is able to read and interpret the "Writing on the Wall," again because God revealed its interpretation to him.

- **The Fiery Furnace**
  Shadrach, Meshach and Abednego stood firm in their faith even in the face of threatened torture and death. For their refusal to bow to an image they were thrown into a very hot furnace. But rather than being burned to ashes, they were joined by a fourth and emerged unharmed. When King Nebuchadnezzar saw this he cried out: "Look! I see four men walking around in the fire, unbound and unharmed, and the fourth looks like a son of the gods" (Daniel 3:25, NIV). This fourth figure was probably a pre-incarnate appearance of Jesus.
  Jesus promises to never leave us. Even though we and others can't see Him, He is as present to us, all the time, as He was to Shadrach, Meshach and Abednego.

- **Shutting the Mouths of the Lions**
  Now it's Daniel's turn to obey or face torture and death. Jealous men manage to get the king to set up rules about worship, which Daniel cannot obey. The king, who loved Daniel, could not do anything about this—he was trapped into writing the decree. Daniel spends the night in the lion's den and when the king comes to see if he has survived, Daniel replies: "My God sent his angel, and he shut the mouths of the lions. They have not hurt me…"(Daniel 6:22).

- **"Son of Man"**

  In Daniel's dream, recorded in Daniel Chapter 7, he sees "one like a son of man." Further description reveals One who is given "authority, glory and sovereign power."

  The LORD refers to Ezekiel through the book by his name, as "son of man."

  "Son of Man" was Jesus' favorite title for Himself, combining "son of man," as Ezekiel was named, giving the idea of humanity and "one like a son of man," in Daniel, indicating divinity.

- **The Stone**

  Compare Daniel 2:34-35 with Luke 20:17-18. In the Daniel passage King Nebuchadnezzar has a dream about a huge statue made up of different materials. At the end of the dream:

  > a rock was cut out, but not by human hands. It struck the
  > statue on its feet of iron and clay and smashed them.
  > Then the iron, the clay, the bronze, the silver and the
  > gold were broken to pieces at the same time...But the
  > rock that struck the statue became a huge mountain and
  > filled the whole earth
  > (Daniel 2:34-35, NIV).

  Luke 20:17-18 reads: "Everyone who falls on that stone will be broken to pieces; anyone on whom it falls will be crushed."

  Nebuchadnezzar's dream points forward to Jesus Christ. Jesus is the Rock and it is His Kingdom that will ultimately fill the earth.

Redemptive History through Daniel

Daniel and his three friends went into Babylonian exile 19 years before the rest of the population of Judah. These were faithful men and their stories should spur us on to courageous living in hostile situations. Our culture is becoming increasingly hostile to Christianity. "The greatest threat to faithful living is compromise," said Dr. Alvin Padilla, Professor of New Testament, Gordon-Conwell Theological Seminary. There is no compromise on the parts of Daniel, Shadrach, Meshach and Abednego. They held firmly to their faith in perfect trust in the God of the Universe.

Shadrach, Meshach and Abednego answer the king in a most astounding way when threatened with the "fiery furnace." "If we are thrown into the blazing furnace, the God we serve is able to deliver us from it, and he will deliver us from Your Majesty's hand." What a statement of faith and trust!

They go on to add, "But even if he does not, we want you to know, Your Majesty, that we will not serve your gods or worship the image of gold you have set up" (Daniel 3:17-18). [We will not compromise!]

Daniel served or had influence during the administrations of the Babylonian and Medo-Persian Empires. His probable dates of ministry are from 605 BC to 536 BC. Cyrus issued his decree allowing the Jews to return to Jerusalem in 538/537—a year or two before Daniel died.

Daniel, Shadrach, Meshach and Abednego were sent, unwillingly, to gentile nations. There they witnessed to other "nations" about the One True God. The kings who came to seek Jesus at His birth were from the East—had the witness of Daniel and his friends influenced them 500 years before?

The events and prophecies in the book of Daniel are to be an encouragement to the Hebrews about to face exile and life away from Jerusalem. The lives of the faithful four give us models of how to live in a hostile culture. The prophecies remind us that our God is a Sovereign LORD. He knows the end from the beginning and His promises to us are absolutely faithful. There was an end to exile, Jesus Christ did come and He will come again. Ours is to be like Daniel, Shadrach, Meshach and Abednego—to live faithful, courageous, trusting lives before the God of the Universe even in the face of great trials.

Chapter 7

"If I Die, I Die"

Esther Chapters 1-9

Though the cause of evil prosper,
Yet the truth alone is strong;
Though her portion be the scaffold,
And upon the throne be wrong;
Yet that scaffold sways the future,
And behind the dim unknown,
Standeth God within the shadow,
Keeping watch above His own. [8]

Both Jews and Christians raised the question of whether to include the Book of Esther in the Canon of Scripture. One of the reasons against inclusion was because of its total lack of reference to the LORD. It obviously was included and has much to say about the way God can act for His people in providential ordering of events; not always by dramatic miracles. Esther's story probably takes place around 480 BC—some 50 years after Daniel's death.

Questions to ponder as you read the text:

1. Under the Persian King Xerxes (aka: Ahasuerus) why is Queen Vashti deposed? (Esther 1:10-12).

---

[8] James R. Lowell, "Once to Every Man and nation" (No. 463) in *Hymns for the Living Church* (Carol Stream, Illinois; Hope Publishing, 1980).

2. Read Esther 2:5-7. What was Mordecai's relationship to Esther?

   **Trace Mordecai's genealogy. Of which King of Israel was he a direct descendant? (Esther 2:5 and 1 Samuel 9:1-2).

3. How does Esther become Queen? (Esther 2:8-18).

4. What precipitates Haman's murderous intent? (Esther 3:1-6)

5. Haman is an "Agagite". It is very likely that he is directly descended from Agag king of the Amalekites. Take time to review the last confrontation between the house of Saul and the house of Agag (1 Samuel 15:7-9). It is very likely that some of the Amalekites were "spared"—although Samuel killed King Agag. Thus six centuries later these 2 ancient enemies met again—Mordecai and Haman.

6. What is "Haman's edit" and how does he obtain it? (Esther 3:8-15).

7. What does Mordecai want Queen Esther to do? How does she respond? (Esther 4:3-16).

8. What does Esther request of the king? (Esther 5:1-8).

9. Whose suggestion is it to have Mordecai killed immediately? (Esther 5:9-14).

10. That night—between Esther's two banquets—the king can't sleep. The book of the chronicles of his reign is brought to him and he reads about the foiled plot intended to kill him (Esther 2:21-23). Belatedly the king announces honor for Mordecai who foiled the assassination plot. What does the king plan and who is assigned to carry it out? (Esther 6:4-10).

11. How does Haman fall into his own trap? (Esther chapter 7).

12. How do Mordecai and Esther save their people? (Esther 8:1-8).

13. ***Both Queen Vashti and Queen Esther challenge a command of the king—why the very different outcomes?

14. ***As you reflect on the Scripture from this section, do you note any hint, type, or foreshadow of Jesus Christ?

NOTES

What do we learn about Jesus in the Book of Esther?

Mentioned in the introduction was the fact that the name of God or "The LORD" is never mentioned in this book. But Jesus is very much present throughout this book because Jesus is the Lord of coincidence. All of these coincidences are not just chance—rather they are all God orchestrated.

"Coincidences" in the Book of Esther:

- **Esther was picked from among many to become Queen**
  Among all the many beautiful young women, Esther just happened to be chosen by the king.

- **The king extends the scepter to Esther**
  Mordecai asked Esther to go to the king and pled for the lives of her people—the Jews. But the law states that anyone who approaches the king without being summoned will be killed—unless the king extends his gold scepter. Esther had not been summoned for a month. However, when Esther appeared, the king just happened to be pleased with Esther and extended the scepter.

- **The king's sleepless night**
  Esther's request is for the king and Haman—the one who wanted to murder all the Jews—to come to her banquet. The night before the banquet the king just happens not to be able to sleep. In his reading of the chronicles of his reign he just happens to read about how Mordecai revealed a plot to kill the king, thus saving the king's life.

- **Haman happened to be in the court**
  The king finds that Mordecai has never been honored for protecting the king. The king asks for whomever is in the court to do that honoring. Haman—the archenemy of the Jews, just happens to have entered and has to honor rather than kill his enemy.

- **Haman named as the Jewish threat**
  On the second night of the banquet Queen Esther gives for the king and Haman, she identifies herself with the race of people that Haman is planning to destroy. But it just happened that since the king had so recently honored the Jew Mordecai he realizes that he has been pulled into a trap of Haman's planning.

- **Haman caught in his own trap**
  The king steps out of the room and Haman falls into Esther's lap to plead for his life. The king just happens to come back at that moment and thinks Haman is trying to rape the Queen. And so Haman is put to death on the gallows he had set up to kill Mordecai.

All of these events had to happen and in the timely manner in which they did in order for the Jews to be saved from slaughter. Only our LORD could have orchestrated all of this. God does at times, stand in the shadows keeping watch above His own.

Redemptive History through Esther

Some commentators talk about the continuing battle between the two seeds (Genesis 3:15)—the godly seed and the seed of the serpent. This is an ongoing battle but we know who wins; we're told that in the Genesis passage. Ultimately one will have his head crushed while the other suffers a significant, but not a fatal wound.

In the Book of Esther this particular chapter of the battle is between Mordecai and Haman but dates back centuries. Deuteronomy 25:17-19 says:

> Remember what the Amalekites did to you along the way
> when you came out of Egypt. When you were weary and
> worn out, they met you on your journey and attacked all
> who were lagging behind; they had no fear of God. When
> the LORD your God gives you rest from all the enemies
> around you in the land he is giving you to possess as an
> inheritance, you shall blot out the name of Amalek from
> under heaven. Do not forget! (NIV).

God judged Amalek and ruled death for them because of their excessive evil. King Saul took it upon himself to pardon some Amalekites (1 Samuel 15) and thus many years later—Haman. Haman was a descendant of Amalek; Mordecai a descendant of King Saul.

As we know, this was not the only time in history that someone has tried to annihilate the Jews. The Book of Esther is a powerful reminder that God is in control of History and He is able to deliver and protect His people.

> Waiting for justice to be done is one of the hardest aspects
> of life in our fallen world. So often, we see the righteous
> trodden underfoot and the enemies of our LORD

ascendant, and this might tempt us to wonder if things will
ever be set right. [9]

It takes only a small amount of time to read through the Book of Esther. But in the book we are reading about many, many years of Mordecai, Esther and the Jews being trodden underfoot. No doubt Mordecai thought that his lot would not change in his lifetime, but then, in a moment things turned upside down. "Although the wicked may seem to meet with great success, from the vantage point of eternity, it is only fleeting." [10] May the Book of Esther be a reminder to us that God will right all wrongs, there will be an end to suffering, sin and death—some day, and we will be in the presence of our LORD forever. All this because Jesus Christ, our LORD, willingly took our place on the scaffold and laid down His life in payment for our redemption.

Take time to praise and worship our majestic King.

---

[9] *Tabletalk Magazine,* Ligonier Ministries, August 13, 2015, 44.
[10] Ibid, 44.

Chapter 8

Return to Jerusalem – Temple

Ezra 1:1-8; 2:68—7:28; 8:15—10:17

I rejoiced with those who said to me, "Let us go to the
house of the LORD"
(Psalm 122:1, NIV).

Daniel may have been around 80 years old when Cyrus issued his decree allowing the Jews to return to Jerusalem. In Daniel Chapter 9 we read the faithful, humble prayer of one of the LORD's most trusting servants—Daniel. Daniel realizes that the 70 years of exile, predicted by Jeremiah are about finished (Jeremiah 25:11-12; 29:10). He also realizes that the hearts of the people have not changed. Nonetheless he pleads with the LORD for the return of the captives to Jerusalem; A most eloquent prayer. Shortly after this prayer is uttered, Cyrus issues his decree. We'll pick up the story in the Book of Ezra.

Questions to ponder as you read the text:

1. What prompted King Cyrus to write his decree? (Ezra 1:1).

2. What was included in the decree of Cyrus? (Ezra 1:2-4).

3. What motivated those who left Persia to go back to Jerusalem? (Ezra 1:5).

4. What was the first thing done by those returning to Jerusalem? (Ezra 3:1-2).

5. What does Ezra 3:3 tell us about conditions in Jerusalem?

People returning from Persia had been away from Jerusalem for as long as 70 years. They are strangers to the land. During their time away, "outsiders" plus some from the old northern kingdom have settled Jerusalem and environs. These people are resentful of the return of the Jews.

6. Chapters 4-6 describe some of the opposition faced by those trying to re-build the Temple and the wall. Chapter 4:1-5 and 4:24 apply to the building of the Temple. Chapter 4:6-23 applies to attempts to re-build the wall. The opponents of the Jews sent several letters to the various kings of Persia trying to stop building of any kind. In the letter written to King Artaxerxes what do those opposed to the Jews accuse them of? (Ezra 4:12-16).

7. What is the response from the King? (Ezra 4:19-22).

8. Building of the Temple is stopped for 10 years. When the Jews again begin work on the Temple, once more those in opposition try to discourage them and write a letter—this time to King Darius. They ask that a search be made to see if there was a decree from King Cyrus authorizing the re-building of the Temple. What is King Darius' reply? (Ezra 6:6-12).

9. What is the problem in Ezra 9:1-2? Who were involved as part of the problem?

10. ***Do you see any connection between this issue and what the Apostle Paul has to say in 2 Corinthians 6:14-15?

11. How do the people respond to Ezra's prayer? (Ezra 10:1-4).

12. ***As you reflect on the Scripture from this section, do you note any hint, type, or foreshadow of Jesus Christ?

NOTES

What do we learn about Jesus in the Book of Ezra?

- **Jesus the LORD of history**
  Just before Babylon conquered Judah and took the people captive (exile), Jeremiah 25:11-12 and Jeremiah 29:10 predicts two things (God's promises):

  This whole country will become a desolate wasteland, and these nations will serve the king of Babylon seventy years. "But when the seventy years are fulfilled, I will punish the king of Babylon and his nation, the land of the Babylonians, for their guilt," declares the LORD, "and will make it desolate forever (Jeremiah 25:11-12, NIV).

  This is what the LORD says: "When seventy years are completed for Babylon, I will come to you and fulfill my good promise to bring you back to this place (Jeremiah 29:10, NIV).

  In 639 Cyrus defeats Babylon and sets up the Medo-Persian Kingdom. In 538/7 Cyrus issues the decree which allows the Jews to return to Jerusalem and rebuild the Temple. It was exactly seventy years between the Fall of Jerusalem and the completion of the Temple upon the return from exile. Both of these things, predicted by Jeremiah, were fulfilled: defeat of Babylon and return from exile.

- **Sovereignty and Free Will**
  Jesus is Sovereign over history. Cyrus, Ezra and the people who returned from exile acted out of their own free will as God's providence worked into their lives to bring His plan to fruition.

- **The Patience and Kindness of God**
  In Daniel's prayer (Daniel 9) he recognizes the "great and awesome God, who keeps his covenant of love with all who love

him and obey his commands" (Daniel 9:4). He also recognizes how sinful God's people are. He pleads for God to be faithful to His promise of release from exile after seventy years but he also tells the Lord that he is very aware of the continued sin and disobedience of the Jews (he humbly includes himself in this). He prays about all that the Lord has done, and then says:

> "yet we have not sought the favor of the LORD our God by turning from our sins and giving attention to your truth...yet we have not obeyed him [The LORD]... We do not make requests of you because we are righteous, but because of your great mercy" (Daniel 9:13,14,18).

The Lord was faithful to His promise and allowed those who wanted, to return to Jerusalem. But, they were not obedient—as we've seen in The Book of Ezra. Their hearts were not changed. Once again we see the truth of 2 Peter 3:9 demonstrated.

> The Lord is not slow in keeping his promise, as some understand slowness. Instead he is patient with you, not wanting anyone to perish, but everyone to come to repentance.

Let us not presume on His patience. See the last sentence: "it is His will that we come to repentance." Our hearts need to be changed by the Holy Spirit and we need to confess, repent and trust in Jesus.

Chapter 9

Nehemiah – Return to Jerusalem – Wall

Nehemiah Chapters 1-6

Unless the LORD builds the house, the builders labor in
vain. Unless the LORD watches over the city, the guards
stand watch in vain
(Psalm 127:1, NIV).

Nehemiah's prayer in chapter 1 is very similar to Daniel's
prayer—Daniel 9. Remember Daniel preceded Nehemiah by almost 100
years. (It's worth flipping back and forth between these two prayers to
see their similarity). The LORD grants Nehemiah favor and he sets off
from Susa, in Persia, for Jerusalem.

Questions to ponder as you read the text:

1. What was the state of Jerusalem at the beginning of Nehemiah?
   (Nehemiah1:1-3).

2. What was Nehemiah's response to this? (Nehemiah 1:4).

3. What aspects of prayer can you identify in Nehemiah's prayer? (Nehemiah 1:5-11).

4. What was Nehemiah's request of the King of Persia? (Nehemiah 2:4-8).

5. To what office in Judah was Nehemiah appointed? (Nehemiah 5:14).

6. Two enemies of the Jews are mentioned here. What are their names and how do they view Nehemiah? (Nehemiah 2:10).

7. What does Nehemiah want to do? (Nehemiah 2:17-18).

8. The wall building begins. What kind of hostile opposition did the Jews face (Fill in chart below – all references are from Nehemiah)?

Ref	Opposition	Ref	Response
2:19		2:20	
4:1-3		4:4	
4:7-8		4:9	
6:1-2		6:3	
6:5-7		6:8-9	
6:10		6:11-15	

9. Did the threats of their enemies have an affect on the wall builders? (Nehemiah 4:10).

10. What was Nehemiah's response to their fears? (Nehemiah 4:13-14).

11. What kind of internal conflict do you note? (Nehemiah 5:1-5)

12. How did Nehemiah respond? (Nehemiah 5:6-11).

And what was the result of Nehemiah's admonishment? (Nehemiah 5:12).

Have you faced opposition because of your walk with the Lord?

How do you react?

13. How long did it take to rebuild the wall? (Nehemiah 6:15).

14. ***As you reflect on the Scripture from this section, do you note any hint, type, or foreshadow of Jesus Christ?

NOTES

What do we learn about Jesus in the Book of Nehemiah?

- **Jesus Works in the Hearts of Pagans**
  King Artaxerxes noted Nehemiah's demeanor. The king responds favorably to Nehemiah's requests: to go to Jerusalem, for letters to insure safe-conduct, for supplies to rebuild the wall in Jerusalem, as well as an un-asked for guard to accompany him.

- **Jesus Works in the Lives of Believers - Prayer**
  Nehemiah was constantly in prayer: fully developed prayer (chapter 1 and 9) and many "arrow" prayers: 2:4; 4:9; 5:19; 6:9; 6:14; 13:14; 13:22; 13:29 and 13:31.

- **Blessing and Good Favor**
  Jesus blessed the efforts of Nehemiah and all those working to rebuild the wall. He blessed Nehemiah in his honest, fair, and humble governing.

- **Perseverance**
  The Jews are empowered to persevere even in the face of continued opposition, threats, scheming, mocking, and plots to disrupt. Despite all of these afflictions they re-built the wall in 52 days.

May this book encourage us to faithfully build the walls God calls us to build and may we rely on God to encourage us as He did Nehemiah and the wall builders.

Redemptive History through Nehemiah

Through God-orchestrated great favor from pagan rulers, the Jews are allowed to return to Jerusalem. There, over a period of nearly 100 years they re-build the Temple, the wall around Jerusalem, and the city. All of these endeavors sparked severe opposition from those who did not want the Jews to be back in the land. But because of the LORD's good favor and His faithful promises, their enemies were subdued.

Not only did they face external opposition but also internal rebellion, sin and the constant battle against syncretism. Ezra and Nehemiah worked hard to encourage the reforms needed to secure the well being of the returned exiles so that the nation would enjoy fullness of living.

They needed to build up the population, "The city was large and spacious, but there were few people in it, and the houses had not yet been rebuilt" (Nehemiah 7:4).

"They read from the Book of the Law of God, making it clear and giving the meaning so that the people could understand what was being read" (Nehemiah 8:8). Following this reading, the people committed themselves to the following reforms:

- **Equally Yoked**
  "We promise not to give our daughters in marriage to the peoples around us or take their daughters for our sons" (Nehemiah 10:30). This would not have applied to "foreigners" who had put their faith in the LORD God, like Rahab and Ruth.

- **Sabbath Observance**
  They promised not to buy merchandise on the Sabbath and they promised, "Every seventh year we will forgo working the land and will cancel all debts" (Nehemiah 10:31).

- **The Tithe**

  "We assume the responsibility for carrying out the commands to give a third of a shekel each year for the service of the house of our God..." (Nehemiah 10:32).

Nehemiah left Jerusalem and returned to the Persian Court for a time. During the time he was away many of the promises of the people to obey God's Law, quickly slipped resulting in:

- Accommodation to those antagonistic to the faith
- Not giving the tithe
- Unequal yoking (to name a few)

Thus underscoring the need of the people to have in their presence a strong godly leader encouraging and directing them at all times. Like the period of the judges, their external behavior deteriorated without strong and constant guidance. Again begging the question for us, what do I/we need to stay faithful to the LORD?

Chapter 10

The Sun of Righteousness Will Rise

Chapters 1-4

"For a brief moment I abandoned you, but with deep
compassion I will bring you back. In a surge of anger I hid
my face from you for a moment, but with everlasting
kindness I will have compassion on you," says the LORD
your Redeemer
(Isaiah 54:8-9, NIV).

We are now at the last book in the Old Testament. After Exile did
Israel learn? Are things going better? Is Israel now obedient and trusting
in the LORD? Is all well with their souls?

Questions to ponder as you read the text:

1. In Mercy God brings back some of Israel into The Land, but many have
   not truly repented and changed their hearts to follow the Lord's way.
   At the close of the Old Testament—enumerated by the Prophet
   Malachi—how is Israel doing? Fill in the following chart: list the
   offense confronted by Malachi then note what God intended or how
   does Malachi say the offense needs to be righted? All references are
   from the Book of Malachi.

Ref	Offense	Ref	What was to be/how was it to be corrected
1:6		2:4-7	
2:13-14		2:15-16	
3:5		3:6-7	
3:8-9		3:10a	

2. What is God's promise about the tithe? (Malachi 3:10-12).

Have you seen this principle work in your life? If you have, share this with someone as encouragement to be generous with our resources.

3. In chapter 3:16-4:2 two groups of people are identified. Who comprise each group and what is their fate?

4. What is the final prophecy—the last word from the Old Testament? (Malachi 4:5-7).

5. ***Look at the following references. Identify how each one adds to a growing understanding of the Messiah. (Feel free to add any others you think of.)
   Genesis 3:15

   Genesis 22:8

   Exodus 12:13

   Deuteronomy 18:15-18

2 Samuel 7:16

Psalm 110

Isaiah 7:14

Isaiah 9:6-7

Isaiah 11:1-9

Isaiah 53

Micah 5:2

Malachi 4:5-6

NOTES

Redemptive History through The Old Testament

In the beginning of the story, God created everything "very good." Mankind (male and female) a special creation was made in His—God's image. Their task was to represent the LORD to the entire creation. They were to administer God's rule of harmony, love and justice over all the creation. They were to "rule" as servants not tyrants. But they rebelled against God—trading the law of God for the law of sin resulting in a cosmic tragedy, for it ushered in the reign of Satan.

God started with individuals to build His kingdom but when sin entered, evil spread so rapidly that God responded in judgment with the flood and the judgment at Babel. Then He chose an individual—Abraham, growing into a family then a nation. He spelled out His Law that told them how they were to live in accordance with the way He designed them. He promised blessings for obedience and warned again of death for disobedience. He gave them godly leaders—Moses, Joshua, and some of the judges but when those godly leaders died, the people soon became unfaithful, demonstrating their need for a permanent *righteous* leader. They wanted a king but their choice of a king was not what God knew they needed.

Then God anointed a king "after His own heart," and promised that David's kingdom would be forever, "Your house and your kingdom will endure forever before me; your throne will be established forever" (2 Samuel 7:16, NIV).

God described Himself as Israel's husband but she responded by chasing after other "gods" in spiritual adultery—graphically described as whoredom.

God sent prophets and godly kings to lead Israel back into obedience and to warn, again and again of what would happen with continued disobedience. Finally God's patience ran out and He brought an "evil" nation to carry out the final warning. The final consequence for disobedience was exile from the land of promise.

The prophets also spoke of hope, forgiveness, God's faithfulness and the promise of restoration. Ultimately He would provide a new heart, atonement for all their sin, and resurrection. The prophets also told of a Servant who would be a light to the nations and finally bring them home from exile.

At the end of the Old Testament God had graciously allowed Israel to return to the land but they were still in "exile"—their hearts had not changed. Although God had promised that David's "house" was forever, it looked as if the "tree" of David's house had been felled.

There were, however, tiny sparks of hope; a descendant of David, Jehoiachin had been graciously released from prison by a Babylonian king—the tree was not dead—there was a shoot from that fallen tree and with it hope in the faithful promise of God. Following Daniel's prayer from exile (Daniel 9:24-26), God tells Daniel that further "exile" would happen:

> "Seventy 'sevens' are decreed for your people and your
> holy city to finish transgression, to put an end to sin, to
> atone for wickedness, to bring in everlasting
> righteousness, to seal up vision and prophecy and to
> anoint the Most Holy Place.

Although the meaning of "seventy sevens" is widely debated, God's promise is that there will be an end to sin, atonement made for sin, and everlasting righteousness will prevail—someday.

Following Malachi there were 400 years of prophetic "silence" followed by the appearance of the last Old Testament prophet—John the Baptist who came in the "spirit of Elijah."

Intertestamental Period—400 Years of Silence

The following is a very brief summary of the 400 years between the Old Testament and the New Testament. During this time, the Jews were scattered in Egypt, Persia, Jerusalem (Judah) and elsewhere.

I   Persian Rule – 539-331BC

II Greek Rule – 331-63 BC
    A   The Persians were conquered by the Greeks—Alexander The Great.
       1   There was great influence of the Greek culture upon conquered lands this was known as Hellenization.
       2   Greek became the common language.

    B   323 BC death of Alexander The Great

    C   Ptolemies (Greek generals) ruled Palestine and Egypt
       1   The Jews retained a good deal of freedom to practice their religion.
       2   There was some self-rule under the High Priest.
       3   In about 100 BC, the Old Testament was translated into Greek.
       4   The "Dead Sea Scrolls" were the transcribed work of the Essenes. These scrolls, hidden for centuries, included some of the oldest known manuscripts of the Old Testament. (They were discovered in 1947 AD).

    D   In 198 BC, the Seleucids (Kings of Syria), in particular Antiochus III occupied Palestine.

    E   In 175 BC Antiochus IV–aka Epiphanes came to power in Palestine. His name means "God manifest."

    F   The Romans began to threaten Antiochus.
       1   Antiochus blamed the Jews for his troubles.
       2   Antiochus began religious persecution of the Jews.
         a   Circumcision was not allowed.
         b   Copies of the Law were desecrated.

       c   No Sabbath celebration was allowed.

       d   The Temple was desecrated.

          1   A statue of Zeus was set up in the Temple.

          2   A Pig was sacrificed in the Temple, on the alter.

          3   The Jews were compelled to make sacrifices to Zeus.

G   164 BC – Maccabean revolt

    1   Under the Maccabees the Jews again occupied Jerusalem.

    2   The Temple was re-dedicated.

    3   Celebration of Hanukkah was initiated.

H   164-162 BC The Hasmonean Dynasty (descendants of Maccabees) ruled Palestine.

    1   This unshed in Judean independence.

    2   The Hasmonean dynasty was established.

       a   Sadducees were:

          1   Aristocratic conservative Jews

          2   They supported the Hasmoneans (Maccabees).

          3   They were looking for political stability.

          4   They viewed the Pentateuch as the only authoritative scriptures.

          5   They did not believe in the resurrection—after life.

       b   Pharisees were:

          1   In opposition to the Sadducees.

          2   Protested Hellenization.

          3   They developed an extensive oral tradition.

          4   They were looking to preserve purity of faith through regulations that lowered the "standards of God" and made it look like one could please God by works.

III.   Roman Period 63 BC

   A   The Romans defeated the Hasmonean Dynasty (Maccabees).

   B   General Pompey occupied Jerusalem.

   C   37-4 BC Herod was appointed by Rome as king of Judea.

      1   Herod was an Idumean by birth—from the line of Esau.

      2   He was a Jewish proselyte.

3   He was the Herod of Matthew Chapter 2—at the time of Jesus' birth.
4   He was loyal to Rome.
5   His building projects made him famous in the ancient world.
6   In 20 BC Herod greatly added to or rebuilt the Temple – this project went on for years after his death (see John 2:20).
7   He was known as Herod the Great—because of his projects.
8   His vices overshadowed his virtues.
      a   He was egotistical, jealous, and distrustful.
      b   At times he was a madman.
      c   He murdered some of his own children.

IV.   At the opening of the New Testament – the Jews are:
A   Ruled by a foreign power—Rome.
B   Herod is King of Judea: able but despotic.
C   The Jews were waiting for the coming of "salvation"—their Messiah.

Kings of Israel (Northern and Southern Kings)

Name	Ref	N. King	S. King	Age	Reign (yrs)	Good King	Evil King	Comments
Saul	1 Samuel 13:1 (NIV)							
Ish-Bosheth	2 Samuel 2:10							
David	2 Samuel 5:4							
Solomon	1 Kings 11:6, 42							
Rehoboam	1 Kings 14:21-22							
Jeroboam 1	1 Kings 12:20; 13:33-34; 14:20							
Abijah	1 Kings 15:1-3							
Asa	1 Kings 15:9-14							
Nadab	1 Kings 15:25-26							
Baasha	1 Kings 15:33-34							
Elah	1 Kings 16:8-9							
Zimri	1 Kings 16:15-16							
Omri	1 Kings 16:23-26							
Ahab/Jezebel	1 Kings 16:29-31							
Jehoshaphat	1 Kings 22:41-43							
Ahaziah	1 Kings 22:51-53							
Jehoram (aka:Joram)	2 Kings 3:1-3							
Jehoram (aka:Joram)	2 Kings 8:16-18							
Ahaziah	2 Kings 8:25-27							
Jehu	2 Kings 9:6; 10:29,36							

Name	Ref	N. King	S. King	Age	Reign (yrs)	Good King	Evil King	Comments
Jehoash (aka:Joash)	2 Kings 11:21; 12:1-3							
Jehoahaz	2 Kings 13:1-2							
Jehoash (aka:Joash)	2 Kings 13:10-11							
Amaziah	2 Kings 14:1-4							
Jeroboam II	2 Kings 14:23-24							
Uzziah (aka:Azariah)	2 Kings 15:1-4							
Zechariah	2 Kings 15:8-9							
Shallum	2 Kings 15:13-15							
Menahem	2 Kings 15:17-18							
Pekahiah	2 Kings 15:23-24							
Pekah	2 Kings 15:27-28							
Jotham	2 Kings 15:32-35							
Ahaz	2 Kings 16:1-4							
Hoshea	2 Kings 17:1-2							
Northern Kingdom Conquered by Assyria 722 BC								
Hezekiah	2 Kings 18:1-6							
Manasseh	2 Kings 21:1-6							
Amon	2 Kings 21:19-22							
Josiah	2 Kings 22:1-2							
Jehoahaz	2 Kings 23:31-34							
Jehoiakim	2 Kings 23:36-37							
Jehoiachin	2 Kings 24:8-12							
Zedekiah	2 Kings 24:18-19							
Southern Kingdom Taken captive by Babylon 586 BC								

Genealogy of the Kings of Israel and Judah

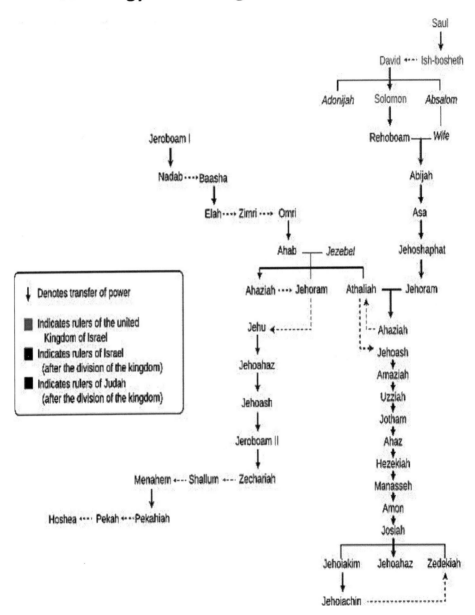

For Further Study

Clowney, Edmund. The Unfolding Mystery Discovering Christ In The Old Testament. Phillipsburg, New Jersey: P&R, 1988. Print.

Dempster, Stephen C. Dominion and dynasty A theology of the Hebrew Bible. Downers Grove, Illinois: Inter Varsity Press, 2003. Print.

Dust To Glory. R. C. Sproul. 1997. DVD. Ligonier Ministries.

Kaminski, Carol. Casket Empty God's Plan of Redemption Through History. Casket Empty Media, 2012. Print.

Made in the USA
Charleston, SC
03 February 2016